CW00486291

Look, Ma! I Did It!

A Perception vs Reality ~~Shitshow~~ Story

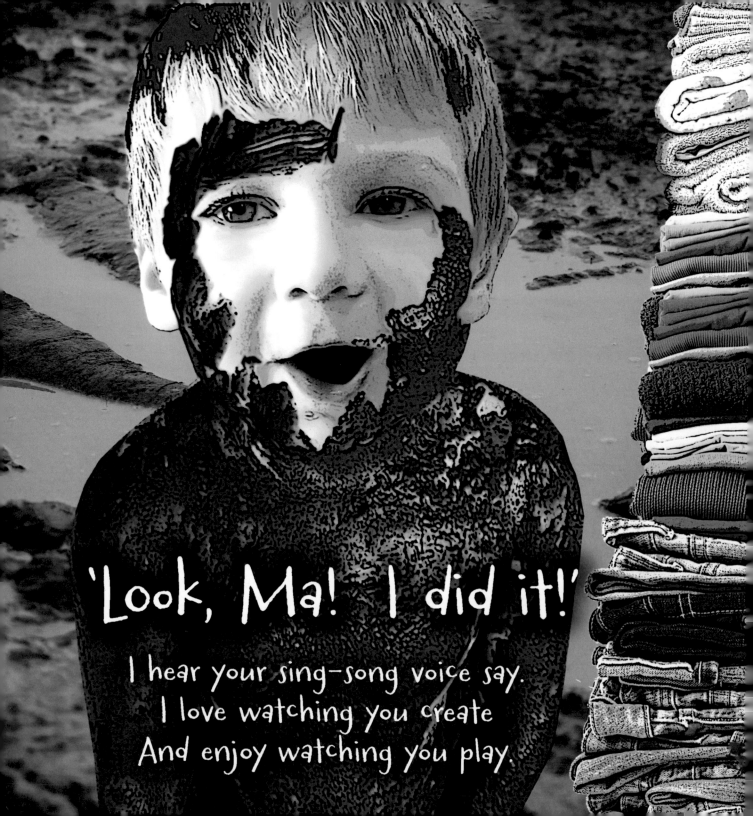

'Look, Ma! I did it!'
I hear your sing-song voice say.
I love watching you create
And enjoy watching you play.

Oh, great. You've created a toy tower with all your dirt-riddled, muddy garden toys. It's toppled over onto the freshly folded, clean piles of washing that I've just spent the last hour f*king folding, in the hopes that - instead of the piles breeding until the entire family has run out of socks and undies - at some point those piles will make their way back into everyone's wardrobes, like some magical Martha Stewart voodoo sh*t.

'Look, Ma! I did it!'

Well, isn't that the sweetest thing?
Interacting with your brother
Really makes my heart sing.

F*cking great. I look away for two seconds
and you've created Baby-in-a-Box,
featuring your six-month-old baby brother,
whose arms are now jammed down by his sides – a
baby-wipes-cardboard-box straitjacket.
And the reason the baby wipes box was empty in the first place?
You've helped yourself to it in the laundry, after you've pulled out
every single f*cking baby wipe from the last remaining packet.

And by 'friends', I mean everyone is f**king
running away from you, because you're now
running naked with s**t up your back
on the top level of a multistorey playground.
I stand on the ground floor looking up,
holding your baby brother and
crying internally, wondering where on earth
you've hidden your pants with the main source
of s**t. Wondering if anyone will notice if I
sneak away and make a quiet exit without you.
I suppose I should be thankful it's not as bad as
the time you s**t down the slide at Maccas, then
proceeded to slide straight down through it,
dragging your waste down the entire length of
the enclosed f**king slide.

'Look, Ma! I did it!'

Your sweet voice cries from afar.
Your confidence is wonderful – and,
This time you've hopped into the car.

I only left the door open because your baby brother was asleep and I'm trying to herd you and your sister back into the house - all of 3.5 metres away. I just want to transfer your baby brother before he hits the next sleep cycle and it's game over - sleep patterns thrown out for the next two f*cking days. But, of course, you've already bolted up the f*cking street, now back into the front of the car, pressing every single button you can find, while your sister has managed to get bitten by an ant and is now howling. 3.5 metres has never felt so f*cking far.

'Look, Ma! I did it!'

Climbing – what fun! A new skill you've mastered.
It's great witnessing you strive,
To reach for what you're after.

Yep, since you've been on the move, you have changed the entire interior design of our f*cking house. Everything is either broken or moved up two metres higher to accommodate the Toddler Factor. Forget minimalism; it's now Nothingalism or Complete F*cking Chaos. No in-between.

And by 'hide', I mean hiding your f*cking hearing aid so I can 'seek' it for the next two days, for the 57,000th time this month. I wonder if we will have to recruit every family member again, just like last time when you pegged it over the fu*king neighbour's fence and we had to break into her back garden because she was away at the time. Then we forgot to reattach the gate latch so her dog escaped and we had a very angry phone call. F*ck's sake; here we go again – the endless search for your hearing aid. Down the lining of the car door, in a ball pit, hidden in the crevice of the couch, pushed carefully under the most heavy piece of furniture, shoved down the drain, to name a few. Your hiding spots become more creative every f*cking time.

'Look, Ma! I did it!'

Nice one, darling! You've done something new. Cleaning your potty into the toilet – well done! Go you!

And then I look closer and see you've also managed to shove in two soft toys, a hat, one of your baby brother's teething toys, and your sister's brand new tap dancing shoes into the bowl BEFORE you put your f**king sh*t and p*ss on top. So there goes the next hour of my life, disassembling your multi-layered sh*t pudding whilst your baby brother screams in the background because he's also due for a feed. Wait - now your sister has joined in on the screaming action too, because she can't find her f**king silver glitter crayon. Let's be honest, it's probably in there too. Or you ate it. For f**k's f**king sake.

'Look, Ma! I did it!'

Testing how something goes together.

Your clever brain never stops Inspecting and studying whatsoever.

How something goes together…also how something comes apart, more to the f**king point. Thank you for investigating how my brand new headphones go together by pulling them apart piece by f**king piece. It's okay, I was only going to take them on my jog tonight – the first opportunity for some downtime in about four years. Back to my exercise and 'me time' being the folding of 33 pairs of socks (87% of which are odd) and doing the sh*t test in all six different pairs of trackie pants that you just had to wear today, now discarded all over the f**king house.

'Look, Ma! I did it!'

You clap your hands with delight.
You've proudly helped your baby brother,
Making sure he is alright.

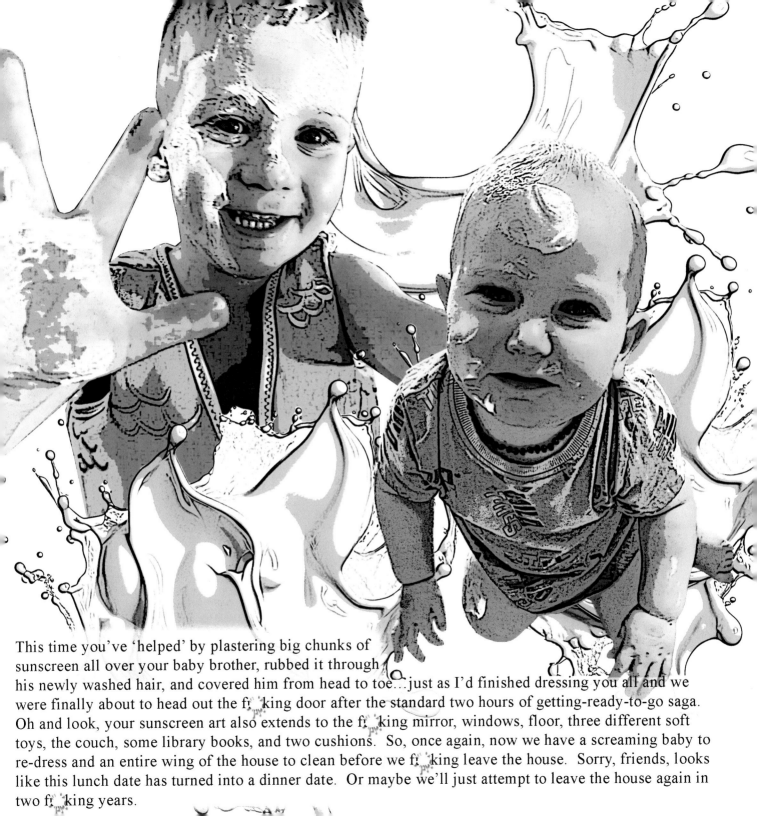

This time you've 'helped' by plastering big chunks of sunscreen all over your baby brother, rubbed it through his newly washed hair, and covered him from head to toe…just as I'd finished dressing you all and we were finally about to head out the fﾟking door after the standard two hours of getting-ready-to-go saga. Oh and look, your sunscreen art also extends to the fﾟking mirror, windows, floor, three different soft toys, the couch, some library books, and two cushions. So, once again, now we have a screaming baby to re-dress and an entire wing of the house to clean before we fﾟking leave the house. Sorry, friends, looks like this lunch date has turned into a dinner date. Or maybe we'll just attempt to leave the house again in two fﾟking years.

And by 'interacting with nature', I mean one second you were gently holding a bug, inspecting him closely, really studying him and giggling sweetly at the sensation of his tickly legs on your hand. Then, next second, you have placed him carefully on the ground…only to start screaming 'DA! DA! DA!' (sounds a lot like another not-so-heartwarming word) as you squish him into the concrete, nothing left but a dark smear on your f*cking death stick. My broken heart sinking then shattering into a thousand pieces as I realise I'm raising a f*cking psychopath.

'Look, Ma! I did it!'

Learning how something works – another new skill.
As you discover,
It really gives me a thrill.

Yes, thrilling that you've managed to open the car door as we go around a f**king roundabout – in this case, the thrill is in the sheer terror of your discovery. The door has flown open and people are beeping their horns at me... because yes, thank you other drivers, the best option for me right now is to stop dead in the middle of the roundabout in peak-hour traffic. And yes, I'm fully aware that my toddler is hanging out of the f**king car because he's obviously figured out how to turn off the child lock when I last had the car door open. Just out for a leisurable stunt drive with my f**king two-year-old. Just a standard day in our household. No f**king worries.

'Look, Ma! I did it!'

You're in the garden helping water plants.
I love little moments like these
That help you advance.

It started off with innocently watering the plants, then the lawn, then the almost dry clothes on the clothesline, then your sister, then spraying me in the f**king face with the hose as I desperately try to grapple it out of your surprisingly strong, vice-like grip. It never ceases to amaze me how everything goes from sweet and innocent to f**king sh*tshow in the space of 2.5 seconds. Every. F**king. Time.

'Look, Ma! I did it!'

Out in the world with my big, brave boy.
Now socialising in public too,
Fearless and full of joy.

Cool, now you've shimmied up to the top of the supporting structure of the playground and gotten your foot stuck in the net.

The 'socialising' I refer to is you screaming, 'IT'S MIIIIIIINE!!!!' at the top of your lungs, so you can be heard from three suburbs away, directed at some poor unfortunate soul who was just trying to climb on the adjacent play equipment. And whose mum is now giving me the stink eye. Yes, obviously everything you touch or look at is yours...but is this not going one step too far when we are talking about 300 sqm of f*king playground? Oh f*k, now you've gotten yourself untangled and I know that look in your eye. You're sizing up the fireman's pole to see if you can fling yourself at it like Basil the F*king Sugar Glider.

Well, that was a fu king mistake. While I sit for the first time since 4 am
(your latest wake up time) for exactly 1 minute 35 seconds, you have managed to pull
the entire coffee caddy off the top of the serving counter where I just bought my coffee,
onto your head. So, in addition to you screaming your head off because the corner has hit you
square in the forehead, the crashing sound as the caddy hits the floor tiles has made everyone
stop dead in their tracks, feel like time stood still, then three people rushed over to help because
coffee, sugar, sweetener, stirrers, and serviettes - and you - have fu king flown everywhere.
Next time, I will not be choosing the most central café in the fu king food court. Noted.
Next time, we will be choosing the outdoor café that is far, far away from everyone.
I wonder if they serve coffee on the fu king moon.

Now you've climbed into bed.
You mumble, 'Wuv you, Ma', snuggle, yawn,
And on my chest you lay your head.

Dammit; you win again. When I'm just about ready to sell you for parts at the end of a very long day, you go and do something stupidly cute and I fall even more in love with you...but not before you elbow me in the face once more, crack yourself up about it, then lick my f ∗king eyeball.

Milton Keynes UK
Ingram Content Group UK Ltd.
UKRC030716280524
443200UK00006B/16